MAY - 5 2016

S0-AEA-930

Shape Hunters

Shapes on the Farm

by Jenny Fretland VanVoorst

Bullfrog Books

Ideas for Parents and Teachers

Bullfrog Books let children practice reading informational text at the earliest reading levels. Repetition, familiar words, and photo labels support early readers.

Before Reading

- Discuss the cover photo. What does it tell them?

- Look at the picture glossary together. Read and discuss the words.

Read the Book

- "Walk" through the book and look at the photos. Let the child ask questions. Point out the photo labels.

- Read the book to the child, or have him or her read independently.

After Reading

- Prompt the child to think more. Ask: Have you ever visited a farm? What shapes did you see?

Bullfrog Books are published by Jump!
5357 Penn Avenue South
Minneapolis, MN 55419
www.jumplibrary.com

Copyright © 2016 Jump! International copyright reserved in all countries. No part of this book may be reproduced in any form without written permission from the publisher.

Library of Congress Cataloging-in-Publication Data

Fretland VanVoorst, Jenny, 1972– author.
 Shapes on the farm / by Jenny Fretland VanVoorst.
  pages cm. — (Shape hunters)
 "Bullfrog Books are published by Jump!."
 Summary: "Carefully leveled text and beautiful full-color photographs take beginning readers on a trip to a farm and encourages them to recognize shapes they see there."—Provided by publisher.
 Audience: Ages 5–8.
 Audience: Grades K to 3.
 Includes index.
 ISBN 978-1-62031-201-8 (hardcover: alk. paper) —
 ISBN 978-1-62031-256-8 (paperback) —
 ISBN 978-1-62496-288-2 (ebook)
 1. Shapes—Juvenile literature.
 2. Farms—Juvenile literature. I. Title.
 QA445.5.F747 2016
 516.15—dc23
                                   2014047133

Series Designer: Ellen Huber
Book Designer: Michelle Sonnek
Photo Researcher: Michelle Sonnek

Photo Credits: All photos by Shutterstock except: iStock, 6, 14–15; Thinkstock, cover, 5, 17, 22bl, 23bl, 23br.

Printed in the United States of America at Corporate Graphics in North Mankato, Minnesota.

Table of Contents

NEXT
2
MILES

Farm Shapes

A farm is full
of shapes.

How many can you find?

3 0053
01086
7847

Kate visits Nana's farm.

Look!

The fields are squares and rectangles.

Look at the barn.

It is painted with shapes.

Red diamonds.

White triangles.

What shape is the door?

It is a rectangle.

The goats stand
in a square.

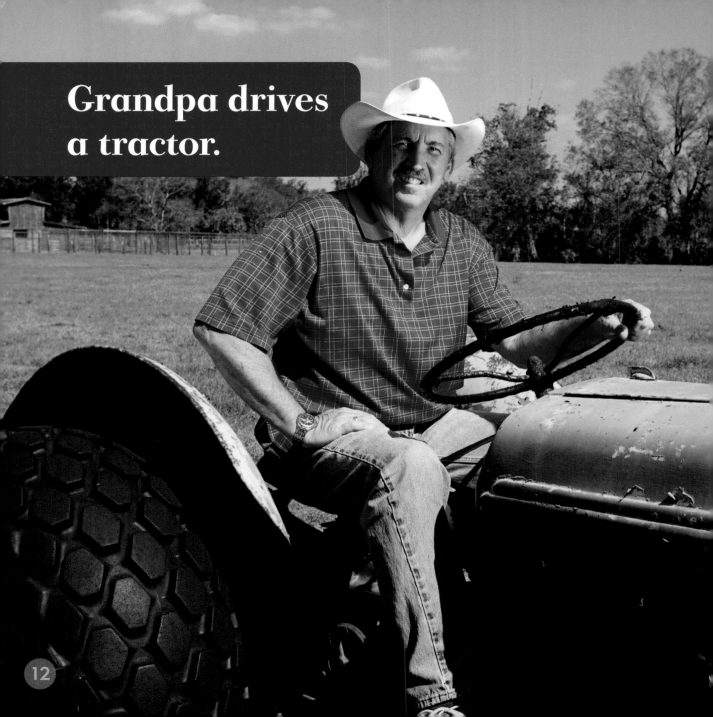

Grandpa drives a tractor.

Each wheel is a circle.

Kate picks berries.

She puts them in a basket.

The opening is a circle.

Nana made cheese.
She used her cows' milk.

She cuts Kate a triangle.
Yum!

This sign is a triangle too.
Watch out for sheep!

Grandpa draws Kate
a picture.

What shape is it?

What does it mean?

More Shapes on the Farm

horseshoe

oval

star

circle

Picture Glossary

barn
A building used for storing farm equipment and housing farm animals.

goat
A hoofed mammal with horns that is often raised for milk or meat.

farm
A piece of land used for growing crops or raising livestock.

tractor
A vehicle with large rear wheels that is used for pulling farm equipment.

Index

To Learn More

Learning more is as easy as 1, 2, 3.

1) Go to www.factsurfer.com

2) Enter "shapesonthefarm" into the search box.

3) Click the "Surf" button to see a list of websites.

With factsurfer.com, finding more information is just a click away.